For friends old and new.

Text and Illustrations Copyright © 2020 by J.L.Cuddehe
All rights reserved. No part of this book may be reproduced, transmitted
or stored in an information retrieval system in any form or by any means,
to include graphic, electronic, mechanical, photocopying, taping
and recording, without prior written permission from the publisher, Found Link Press.

Library of Congress Cataloging Data:

Cuddehe, J.L.
Duck, Duck, Gus / Cuddehe, J.L.
p.30

Summary: A mild-mannered moose named Gus and two endearing,
quirky Ducks are dear friends. Through their adventures together
they model the very best qualities of friendship.
ISBN: 978-0-9836659-8-4
LCCN: 2020907796
1. Moose--Juvenile Fiction, 2. Ducks--Juvenile Fiction, 3. Friendship--Fiction

Illustrations were created using a unique multimedia process
combining watercolor, ink, mastic and digital techniques.

Printed in the USA

20   20   07   1

Found Link Press
13125 Ladybank Lane
Herndon, Virginia USA 20171

Please visit us at: www.FoundLinkPress.com

Duck, Duck, Gus

A Story About Friendship

Words and picures by Judy Link Cuddehe

This is my friend Duck.

And this is my other friend Duck.

Duck and Duck have the same name,

but they are very different.

For example, Duck enjoys imitating machines, animals and opera singers.

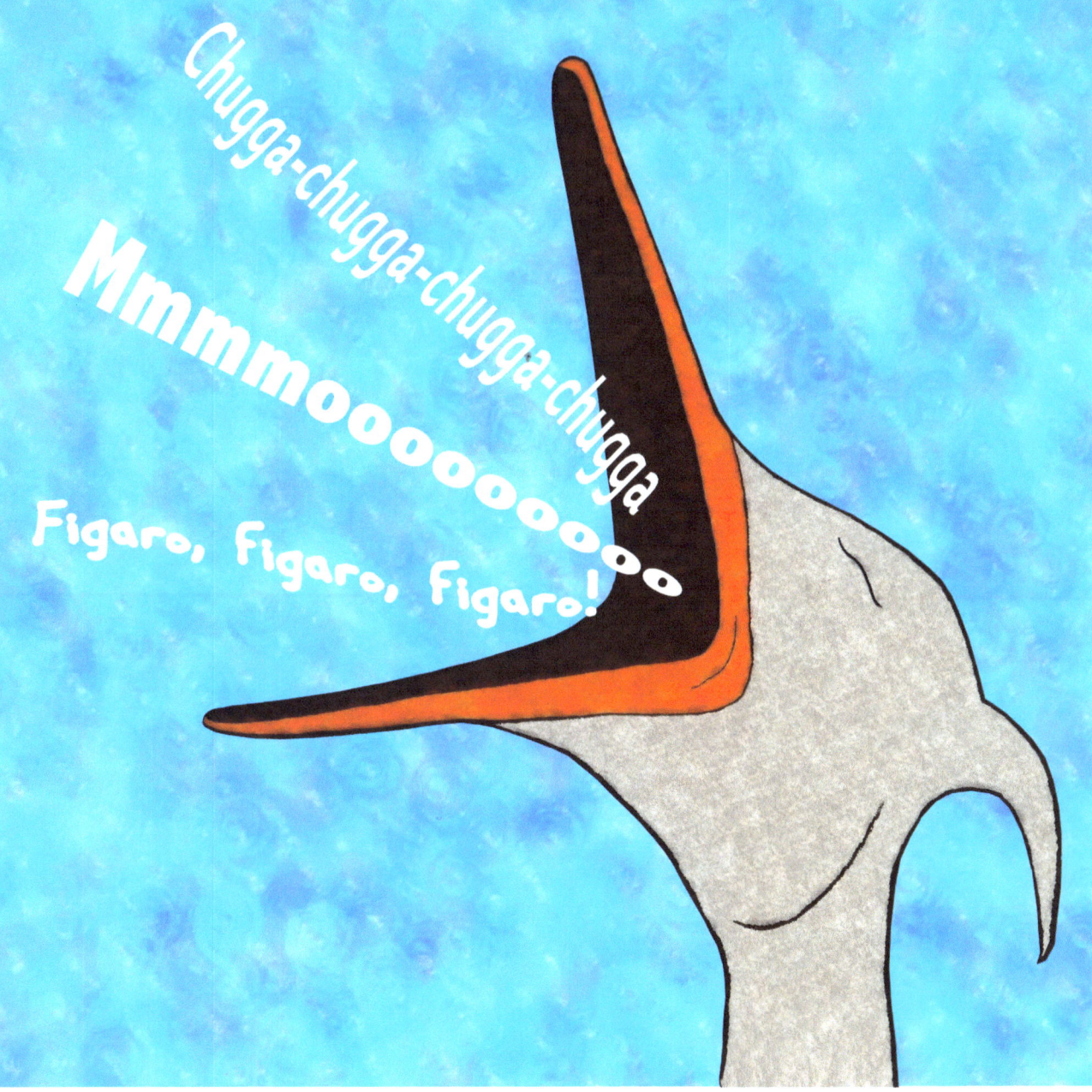

Duck, however, prefers to sit quietly and think. Duck thinks a lot.

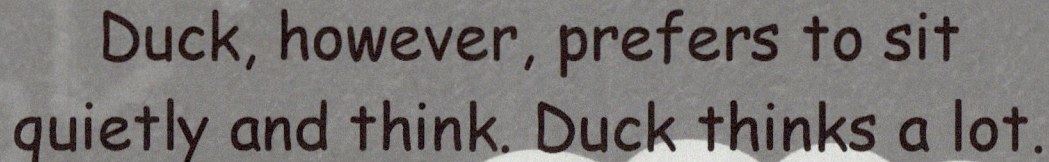

Even so, we are all good friends.

Sometimes we are silly.

We encourage each other

to do spectacular things...

that, alone, we think

are impossible.

We are adventurous together.

Sometimes one of us is braver.

Sometimes we hang out with other friends,

but we try to be friendly anyway.

When we disagree we try to understand.

And when we are apart

we hold each other in our hearts,

Printed in the USA
CPSIA information can be obtained
at www.ICGtesting.com
LVHW062003271223
767424LV00006B/80